Carolyn Westbrook

VINTAGE
FRENCH STYLE

Carolyn Westbrook

VINTAGE
FRENCH STYLE

Homes & gardens inspired
by a love of France

PHOTOGRAPHY BY
Keith Scott Morton & Eric Richards

CICO BOOKS
LONDON NEW YORK

I would like to dedicate this book to all the wonderful and talented homeowners who allowed us to photograph their beautiful homes. This book is such a glorious array of personal style that is reflected in each and every home. Each one of my homeowners has a love of vintage and antique items, which is so crucial to making a house a home. I also wanted to include many of my talented friends who had their retail spaces shot for the Masters of Art chapter. Creating a retail space that customers clamor to see is definitely an art, and I consider these friends some of the best in the business. So here's to all you lovely people and thank you for making this book more beautiful with your amazing talent:

Courtney Barton
Karen Beach
Leslie and Bill Cornog
Julie Ferrell
Mary Francis
Jennifer and Jim Nicholas
Vincent Peach
Jennifer and Dee Pepper
Jonathan Pierce
George Brownlee
Darrel Davenport
Donna Corr of Corrabelle Rose
Ed Fulkerson and Michael Brennan
   of Leftovers Antiques
Jodi and Mike Roberts of Roberts Antiques

Published in 2018 by CICO Books
An imprint of Ryland Peters & Small Ltd
20–21 Jockey's Fields
London WC1R 4BW

341 E 116th St
New York, NY 10029

www.rylandpeters.com

10 9 8 7 6

Text © Carolyn Westbrook 2018
Design and photography © CICO Books 2018

A CIP catalog record for this book is available from the Library of Congress and the British Library.

ISBN: 978 1 78249 548 2

Printed in China

MIX
Paper from responsible sources
FSC
www.fsc.org   FSC® C106563

Editor: Gillian Haslam
Designer: Louise Leffler
Photographers: Keith Scott Morton and Eric Richards

Art director: Sally Powell
Production manager: Gordana Simakovic
Publishing manager: Penny Craig
Publisher: Cindy Richards

CONTENTS

INTRODUCTION 6

PART ONE

HOMES & GARDENS

CHAPTER 1 MAISON 12

CHAPTER 2 MID-CENTURY MODERN 42

CHAPTER 3 CHÂTEAU 58

CHAPTER 4 FARMHOUSE 80

CHAPTER 5 EQUESTRIAN 114

PART TWO

DETAILS & VIGNETTES

CHAPTER 6 TRAYS & TABLETOPS 132

CHAPTER 7 MASTERS OF ART 140

ACKNOWLEDGMENTS 158

INDEX 160

INTRODUCTION

⋘◆⋙

When we first began discussing this book and the direction it should take, we debated the title and thought why not combine my three loves—vintage, French, and style? Everyone can appreciate great style and whether that style is home or fashion, high or low, there is nothing that sets you apart like a vintage piece. Vintage has to be hunted down and found, not just plucked from a rack or off a shelf at your local discount store. It is inspired, not mass produced, and you cannot help but notice and appreciate the detail from the past. When it comes to detail, this is a concept that is well understood by the French.

I was raised with a passion and appreciation for detail, that is reflected in our country home. Tucked away amongst a copse of oak trees, the tale of how we found and renovated the house is quite a story in itself. It began many years ago when we pulled up to an old, dilapidated southern plantation in this small Texas town out in the middle of nowhere. The roof sagged sadly above the enormous columns, but you could tell that it had once been a grand mansion. Despite the peeling paint and the lack of any kind of landscaping, all I could see was potential, while all my husband saw was work! That was the beginning of a new life for us, leaving the big city in our rearview mirror as we headed out down the long dusty road with a huge renovation project ahead of us. The plantation house became the home where our children were raised and is now home to our menagerie of pets, and the landscape is ever-changing.

As you may already know, I was born into the world of design. My mother was a designer and an artist, and throughout my childhood our life was about creating, no matter if it was a garden or re-creating a room environment.

It was a very inspired life and for a child it was an endless education, as our house could change overnight from an Asian-inspired style to contemporary décor. I was taught the importance of an eclectic mix, along with the fact that you had to have vintage pieces in your design plan. The patina of an old piece cannot be faked and while new is nice, all new is cookie cutter.

I instantly fell in love with France on my first trip there. My childhood had taught me a love of French pieces and French style, but I was not prepared for the beauty to be found in an everyday object due to the detail that went into making it. It is not only the design, but the lifestyle that I so admire. The pace is slower and each day is appreciated, along with those who share it with you. Afternoons and evenings are spent in impromptu gatherings with a bottle of wine, a tablecloth thrown across just about anything outdoors, and a colorful salad served with freshly baked bread, and there you have it... a gathering of family and friends. The sound of shared laughter and leaning back in your chair feeling truly relaxed, while enjoying the moment—that is a blessing in itself.

I found inspiration everywhere I visited in France, and was determined to bring that feeling and style back with me. Although my books are eclectic, as I am never about just one style, I do love and appreciate all kinds of beautiful things. I tell my children that I am all about creating beauty.

OPPOSITE: I love the drama that blue and white create in any room. In our historic home the hallways are 20 feet wide and 40 feet long, so it makes for lots of room to design. My favorite hydrangea is oversized and in a wonderful shade of blue that complements the blue-and-white pottery and accents.

Your home is your haven and should reflect and celebrate your own personal history and be filled with objects you adore. That is the beauty of home and for that reason no two homes are the same. As you open the door, relax, and breathe deeply, you are comforted simply by being home. It is important to "nest" and create a home that you wish to be enveloped in. And so begins the hunt for vintage treasures that speak to you, and if they happen to be French, then all the better.

When in France, I can be found wandering through the brocantes and flea markets—an activity that just has to be added to your bucket list. Strolling by the River Seine while perusing the stalls selling old art prints and books is a wonderful thing to do. I love to buy a loaf of bread from a boulangerie and munch on it as I walk down the street, always looking up at the spectacular architecture.

However, despite my love for Paris, as I drive down the gravel road back home, there is no other place that I would rather be. As my lab meets me on the road and leads the way down the driveway with his tail wagging, I laugh to myself. The oak trees canopy the house and I can see the vegetable garden in the distance. My mind flashes back to the beginning, when the house looked as though it would collapse and there was not a speck of landscaping or a flower anywhere. I see how the place has been transformed after a tremendous amount of work, but totally worth it as now it looks like the house I envisioned in my head the very first time I saw it. Our arrival meant that the house had life breathed back into it, and now it will carry on for generations.

Our home is featured in Part One of this book, alongside nine other homes. This book contains many versions of French style—from the sophisticated city elegance of Paris to the grander château style found in country homes, from mid-century modern to simpler farmhouse style. Each style is as wonderful as the others, and each displays a masterful mix of new and vintage. A home should speak of the person or people who dwell there, where they have traveled, where their passion lies, and that can be glimpsed as you open the door. Like an artist faced with a blank canvas, you create your own masterpiece by adding and mixing until it is just right... for now. I say that because my home is constantly changing as I add new vintage finds to the mix, change fabrics and paint colors, and rearrange furniture. I can pick out any object in my home and tell you where it came from, and I always remember what I paid for it.

Part Two of the book is the Details & Vignettes section. The chapter on Trays & Tabletops celebrates the use of trays in serving and decorating, and is an inspiring visual tutorial on creating beautiful tray art. The final chapter, Masters of Art, is inspired by my friends in the design and antiques business, with photos celebrating their stores and booths, and their passion for design. I love the inspiration and ideas that will help you to find solutions for those tough-to-decorate niches, mantels, or tabletops. For those of us who love the art of creating our own vintage over-the-top retail displays (or masterpieces, as I like to call them), this chapter is for you. These are some of the experts and their vision for vignettes is absolutely breathtaking.

I hope this will be a book to savor and will provide you with inspiration to create your own masterpiece—after all, there is no place like home.

XO Carolyn

OPPOSITE: A very feminine chicken house, that is also home to a couple of roosters and the lady turkey, Gloria (she can be seen on page 93). Vintage architectural columns line the path and make for a dramatic entry. A scalloped trim on the roofline and the pink accents create pretty perfection.

PART ONE

HOMES & GARDENS

This section of the book features ten beautifully photographed homes, all displaying their own take on French style. Some are sleek, elegant, and modern, while others are farmhouse-style and filled with vintage charm, but each home is inspiring and bursting with character.

CHAPTER 1 MAISON 12

CHAPTER 2 MID-CENTURY MODERN 42

CHAPTER 3 CHÂTEAU 58

CHAPTER 4 FARMHOUSE 80

CHAPTER 5 EQUESTRIAN 114

CHAPTER 1 MAISON

THE HOMES IN THE MAISON CHAPTER ARE ALL QUITE LARGE AND ALL EXHIBIT A BEAUTIFUL STYLE, BUT AT THE SAME TIME ARE LIVED-IN AND COMFORTABLE.

Some are more French than others, but all are well done and all the owners know how to make you feel at home, which is the essence of the meaning of the word. If you study these homes, you will see they all share the basic decorating strategy that I embrace. First, they all feature vintage pieces. That is my number one rule—I do enjoy new things, but there has to be a vintage mix or a mix of styles and vintage. I do not enjoy a house decorated solely in one style; it has to be an eclectic mix to avoid being stuffy. Second, it has to tell a story—of your travels, your interests, and items you have picked up along the way that are meaningful remembrances of a happy vacation, a beloved time spent in Europe, or a jaunt through a flea-market field.

ABOVE: Something as simple as a magnifying glass can be turned into an extraordinary collection of different types. Here you see vintage and newer versions, some made of horn, others in metal, wood, and enamel. They are arranged in a most interesting way as a tabletop collection in this hallway, and something to gaze upon as you enter the house.

OPPOSITE: The gentle curve of the staircase makes for a perfect nook for the skirted round table that hugs the curve and softens the room. An ornate French armoire makes the perfect hallway piece for storing guests' coats.

All these homes possess good pieces of furniture in neutral colors. When it comes to large pieces, I prefer a neutral palette to give them longevity. Vintage oil paintings, framed botanicals, and antique mirrors are all great for adorning walls. Notice that these all have a favored patina and an aged finish that cannot be bought at a big box retail store. I am not a fan of going to a discount store and buying something just to fill a space on the wall. Think about how many times you are going to look at that wall—it should be something that makes you feel good every time you walk into the room, so it is worth waiting to find just the right piece.

The rooms in this chapter are filled with old books, beautiful urns and planters, and statuary, along with some new pieces added in along the way. It needs to be a mix of you and your family to truly make for a style that is individual to you. Maison is a grand and gorgeous style that offers us much visual inspiration. In this chapter we are allowed a peek into these grand spaces and can live vicariously through these pages.

In this first home, just outside the back door is a perfectly decorated patio that can be used as an outdoor dining space and is decorated with the same care as you would lavish on the interior of the home. An antique mirror is placed above a fabulous French table and reflects the hydrangea blooms and urns beautifully, as well as the chandelier that sits over the large outdoor table. Outdoor living is really an expansion of your home, which means that you can use outdoor rugs, chandeliers on covered porches, oil paintings, lamps, and ceiling fans for comfort. In my own home (featured on pages 58–71), pillows and décor change with the season in our outdoor areas. Likewise, the French feel of these homes spills outside, echoing the style of the interiors.

OPPOSITE: Elegance can be transported to an outdoor dining area, and in a warm climate these spaces can be used for much of the year. The concrete books that are reminiscent of old book bindings are quite a find, and so practical for outdoor decorating. Urns, flowers, plants, and statuary are a must-have in your outdoor spaces.

ABOVE: This small French table has a French barometer adorned with fabulous detail hanging above it. The collection of vintage purple glass bottles is enhanced by the purple blossoms spilling from the vase.

ABOVE: A close-up view of the botanical wall art. An herberie is a collection of pressed herbs under glass, and here it hangs above the chest, filling the niche next to the fireplace. The perfectly aligned frames are in similar soft shades of pale gray.

ABOVE: This is the epitome of a French dining room, but done in a clean, fresh way with white slipcovered chairs surrounding a large dining table capable of hosting a big party. A magnificent fireplace warms the room during the winter months so that guests can dine by the soft glow of a roaring fire. A pretty chandelier overhead adds to the twinkling light. Sprays of pure white orchids and a sleek linen table runner complete the scene.

Fresh flowers and plants are an important element of any room, and this bouquet of peonies, roses, hydrangeas, and chrysanthemums with just a whisper of color does not disappoint.

ABOVE: A very refined antique French bust of a young boy is in amazing condition and adds a touch of vintage beauty to the room. The plinth underneath gives it just enough lift to make it a statement piece. Vintage statuary is often a work of art in itself, and the more detailed, the better. Notice the exquisite detail found in the face of this boy.

OPPOSITE: A finely carved French desk is absolutely the focal point in this home office. It anchors and defines the space, and is complemented by a lovely curved chest and a more modern lamp that show a great mix of new and old. Shelving provides essential storage for books and a great canvas for displaying treasured finds and family photos.

HERE WE VISIT ANOTHER HOME, AND ONE
THAT I FEEL DEFINES THE WORD "MAISON." ALTHOUGH
LARGE, IT IS WELCOMING AND INVITING.

Guests who enter through the back door are first greeted with this mud room, where there is plenty of well-planned, capacious storage for rain boots, hats, and coats, as well as a place to sit while you remove your shoes. This is a house that is really a home, and while it is sophisticated, it has a comfortable and relaxed atmosphere that you notice the instant you walk through the door.

LEFT: A gorgeous grouping of antique brown transferware trays cleverly encircle the vintage ship mirror, which reflects the kitchen beyond. The transferware collection is continued underneath, and stacks of vintage books add to the nod to brown with their vintage leather bindings, embossed with gold type.

OPPOSITE: Pretty striped, ruffled pillows sit atop this precious striped ticking mattress-style cushion and greet you as you walk through the door. Hooks are ready to take totes and bags, while a shelf shows off a vintage yard-long print of roses and makes a great place to drop your hat.

RIGHT: This is the perfect kitchen, with great attention paid to every last detail. The magnificent heavy iron French doors open up to the patio and the table just beyond, for outdoor meals on sunny days. The enormous bar —a huge and beautiful slab of marble with a honed finish—can seat many for indoor dining, and there is also a small table with four upholstered chairs for more formal meals. The lighting over the bar makes a spectacular statement, while the farmhouse sink and the restaurant-style faucet are perfect for a family that really loves to cook and entertain—this is a gorgeous setting for creating culinary delights. Meanwhile, the dog snoozes on a comfortable woven rug that adds texture to the highly polished floor.

OPPOSITE: A closer look at the fireplace mantel that sits opposite the cow painting shown above. The owner's love of brown transferware, as seen on page 20, echoes throughout the house and the tureen shown here is another vintage find, proudly displayed front and center. The French sconces, decked with crystal jewels, were probably picked up at a French flea market and add a touch of beauty and contrast to the hard surface of the mantel.

ABOVE: A gorgeous living area waits just inside the door with a glowing fire and a wonderfully eclectic mix of furnishings and accessories. A huge and fabulous vintage cow painting is the centerpiece on the wall and is flanked by two modern lamps. The vintage zebra rug is a great addition to any room, and the muted fabric of the curtains gives this room a soft sophistication. The woven carpet is custom-made to hug the curve of the stairs and the fireplace, while adding texture and warmth to the room. All these elements combine to make a stunning visual impact on anyone who drops in.

On the other side of the entry hall you are greeted by this stunning French-style dining room. I adore the plate rack, which reminds me of one I glimpsed in a favorite movie. The French chandelier, with its beautiful crystal beadwork that loops elegantly and glistens when illuminated, is the perfect contrast to the warm wood of the farmhouse-style harvest table and bench seating. The drapes in a subtle, muted fabric mirror the window dressing across the hallway and tie the rooms together. A European clock marks time in the corner while a small buffet is tucked away on the other side of the window, and it all comes together in a balanced and wonderful mix of style.

ABOVE: Who wouldn't want to sit down to dinner here, surrounded by the glow from a shimmering French chandelier, the warmth of the wood of a farmhouse table, a prized petite oil painting that peeks from a corner of the room, and comfy linen-covered captain's chairs for the two heads of the table.

OPPOSITE: The built-in plate rack offers a lovely way to display platters of all different shapes and sizes. Again, the homeowner shows off her passion for the favored brown transferware that she had so much fun collecting on her jaunts through the flea-market fields to find her prizes. The eclectic mix of ironstone transferware is brilliant and interesting with rectangles, scalloped edges, and ovals all grouped together to please the eye.

I have always loved beautiful bedding, which is why I began creating my own line of bedding years ago. There is nothing as beautiful as the look and feel of white linen and when layered with vintage pieces, it makes for the ultimate bedroom.

OPPOSITE: White can have such a powerful impact on a bed, and with the absence of color one can really appreciate the fresh, clean beauty that the various textures offer. Vintage lace and embroidered pillows set off by dainty ruffles add a feminine touch to the chrome brad detail on the headboard. All rooms need vintage elements to make them interesting. The bedroom is no different—the Italian metal lamp adds a vintage detail and just a hint of pastel color for a subtle beauty.

ABOVE: Who would not want to take a dip in this tub— it is just begging for a bubble bath. This bathroom has a clean, crisp, spa-like feel, which is what one strives for when creating a bathroom where one can relax and linger. Marble of all kinds can be found here, including the patterned floor that looks as though one is stepping out on to a rug when exiting the tub, while a pristine antique chandelier glows from above for the perfect romantic ambience.

AS WE STEP THROUGH THE
DOORWAY OF THE NEXT HOUSE,
WE CAN IMMEDIATELY SEE THAT
THE HOME BELONGS TO A LOVER
OF VINTAGE AND ART.

You can also see the over-riding attention to detail and the wonderful sense of style that went into making this home. New pieces and antique treasures have been skillfully partnered, with vintage touches layered in to create a very personal and stylish home. Each item has been carefully curated to ensure that it is displayed to best advantage, while thousands of pounds of marble were transported across the globe to create beautiful fireplaces, countertops, floors, and exterior fountains for this fabulous maison.

OPPOSITE: An antique chest with a gorgeous burled wood and contrasting black finish makes for a grand entrance into the home. The chest is an amazing place to show off treasured art pieces that sit atop it and hang on the wall over it. All these pieces are carefully chosen for each room and each space so that it all adds up to perfection.

ABOVE: I do love a fireplace, although a mantel can be a bit tricky to decorate. However, you really cannot go wrong with a mirror over the mantel because it not only reflects the room but also enhances the lighting. Layering a small painting over the mirror adds more interest, and small books, statuary, and candles are always a good idea for a mantel space.

The whole upper floor of this house was designed and planned around this pair of unbelievable stained-glass windows. The color palette of the textured glass is a gentle mix of sea greens, rich teal, soft blue, and deep indigo.

Now this is what I would think of when I picture a bathroom in a maison—a tub fit for a queen! The oversized stained-glass windows flank either side of the tub, which is set off by the marble surround. The antique glass offers an amazing palette of color, especially when caught in sunlight, and at night the spectacular size and beauty of the chandelier make the glass glow. Glimmering sconces are positioned on either side of the window and provide a softer light when the chandelier is not in use. A stack of white fluffy towels offers a soft and luxurious feel, along with the gorgeous pastel rug, picking up on the colors of the glass, which allows you to step out of the tub in comfort, rather than having to tread on a cold, hard floor with wet feet. At the window, soft folds of fabric can be lowered for privacy. This is truly a bathroom you could linger in for hours.

OPPOSITE: The plump, velvet-covered cushioned chairs sit ready and waiting for someone to relax and sip an indulgent glass of Champagne while the bath water runs. I for one would be happy to be surrounded by the beauty of this room at any time of day, and not just at bath time! The dressing area just beyond leads into this area, providing a useful staging post and somewhere to take a seat in between trying on clothes.

I always love a little Asian style thrown into the mix, as it offers a striking contrast to the vintage pieces. This piece of orange chinoiserie ("chinois" is French for Chinese) makes for an amazing entrance hall, adding to the sense of grandeur supplied by the sheer size of the room and the grand piano. The burnt orange color and gold detailing are beautifully set off by the gleaming polished black surfaces of the piano. The chinoiserie cabinet is filled with a delightful selection of little trinkets and treasures that were found while on trips to Asia and brought back to remind the owners of their pleasant travels through the beautiful landscapes.

OPPOSITE: The chinoiserie cabinet is a striking piece, and its doors deserve to be left open so that you can fully appreciate the beautifully detailed decoration.

ABOVE LEFT: We come in for a closer look so that each little cubby can be seen. I love the attention to detail on this piece, with the tiny drawers, the trim, and most of all the color. A collection of vintage glassware is showcased here, each one picked up at a different place and each one evoking a memory of where and when the piece was chosen. From stacks of little saucers, cups, and bowls, to miniature figurines, each is a treasured piece.

LEFT: An outdoor room that really is an extension of the home, with a dazzling array of comfortable cushioned seating, verdant plants, and another stunning stone fireplace mantel. Guests can gather around the fire during the winter months and stay toasty while drinking cocktails before dinner or perhaps roasting marshmallows over the fire. In the summer months, under the cooling breeze of the ceiling fan, they are invited to sit and lounge while the water flows lazily from the pond and statue on the far side of this outdoor living area.

RIGHT: My first thought here is what an amazing firewood storage unit. It is totally utilitarian and gives this space texture and interest at the same time. The huge coffee table can be used for serving or display—here, this perfectly curated tabletop is full of interest, heights, and shapes. There is plenty of seating, so if the party spills outside, this is a place to gather in style, while overlooking and appreciating the gardens.

ABOVE: Here we can see the magnificent use of the stone that was shipped across the globe and fashioned into a tiered fountain that fits perfectly into this backyard oasis. The patio steps down to a lower level, where it is covered by a pergola.

LEFT: This is a genius idea—the tiny footprints of the grandchildren cast in concrete surround the entire patio, forming one of the most creative borders I have ever seen. It is not limited to babies' feet, either—the dog's pawprints make the border even more treasured and inspired.

ABOVE: Hydrangeas abound in this climate and surround the entire yard, so everyday bouquets can be gathered and brought inside for impromptu floral arrangements.

Down on the lower level of the patio and nestled in its own little alcove, an upholstered mattress and a plethora of pillows and prints make a pretty swing seat even more comfy and inviting. As one finishes working in the garden, it is almost impossible to pass by this swing without taking a minute to kick off your garden boots and plop down in this garden paradise, while listening to the birds chirping above. In the welcome shade of the pergola and surrounded by lush green vegetation, it is the perfect spot for a moment of reflection, or even an afternoon snooze.

CHAPTER 2
MID-CENTURY MODERN

—«‹‹◆››»—

HAVING GROWN UP IN A MODERN HOME, I LIKE TO INCLUDE
THIS STYLE IN ALL MY BOOKS. THESE TWO MID-CENTURY
HOMES OFFER A STUNNING LOOK AT "MID-MOD" DESIGN.

This first home has absolutely spectacular architecture. The house feels as if you are outdoors, with a ceiling that seems to reach up forever and the spectacular window-over-window design. This home is modern, with a special appreciation of beautiful and special art pieces that add to the interest. When creating a modern look, it is always important to include elements in the room that prevent the modern from appearing cold. This home is immediately made warmer by the wood detail around all the windows, along with the textured rug on the floor. The fireplace is a stunning visual and can warm up this huge space on a winter night. This is a modern-day inspiration.

ABOVE: A mantel can be a tricky place to design, but this one is expertly done and filled with wonderful antique statuary, a French candlestick, and vintage books, with a striking sculpture on the wall above.

OPPOSITE: It feels as though one is in the outdoors when entering this extraordinary mid-century living room. The architecture itself makes the room, and is absolutely breathtaking. The fireplace that seems to come out of nowhere is like none other I have ever seen, and is sure to inspire even those who are not fans of the modern style. The metal chimney suspended above feels like a piece of modern art too.

RIGHT: The sun's rays coming through the enormous bank of floor-to-ceiling windows shine into the room with glorious beams of light that only add to the drama. Built-in pale wood cabinetry warms up the look of the room, and a comfy oversized sofa provides ample seating for family and friends—always an important consideration for a living space.

RIGHT: This is a dining room that makes an incredibly modern statement. The unusual table supports are in the style of tree trunks, almost like a faux bois, and the wonderful oversized light fixture is a conversation piece. The ceiling beams add a great architectural element to the room. The matching armoires show off the size of the room and are topped with aged handmade pottery bowls. A large-scale picture window allows a wonderful view of the beautifully landscaped grounds just outside and allows an abundance of natural daylight to flood into the room.

Carefully selected pieces are key to any modern scheme, and in this room it is all about the single lamp with its studded base and the wall-hung cow skull, which provide a touch of whimsy. The rug warms the room and, as in the dining room seen on the previous pages, the same beams reach down from the ceiling, adding a note of architectural interest as well as mirroring the other side of the room where the dining table is sited. I can appreciate modern style, but for me a room must have pieces of passion that show who lives there, what they care about, where they have traveled, and what they collect. This homeowner is an avid art enthusiast and the walls are filled with art of all kinds, from cow skulls to sculpture to precious paintings.

LEFT: The tufted white couches are amazingly inviting and again offer plenty of seating for a drink before dinner and some conversation in front of the fire. The furniture is an inspired choice and while this is not your typical coffee table, it works wonderfully well in this setting. It plays host to a magnificent natural bowl.

THIS TOWNHOUSE IS HOME TO A FELLOW
DESIGNER AND, AS WITH ALL DESIGNERS,
THERE IS A SIGNATURE STYLE. THE LOVE OF
MID-CENTURY IS EVIDENT HERE, AND IT IS
DONE SO WELL THAT IT IS MOST WELCOMING.

The attention to detail here is amazing, showcasing the homeowners' genuine love for vintage and their innate skill in displaying art, trinkets, and treasures that have been picked up along the way and chosen very carefully, as it is so important to surround yourself with the things you love. This is one reason why it is vital to put together a theme or plan when designing the interior of your home. This is what you will live with every day and just going out and buying all new mass-produced items in one hit makes for a boring, cookie-cutter home that evokes no feeling or emotion. No matter what your chosen style, you need to select items that have value, and I am speaking of emotional value, rather than monetary worth. You want to surround yourself with pieces that recall wonderful memories and special people and hold sentimental value or historic interest.

ABOVE LEFT: Gorgeous marble abounds in this modern kitchen, with the backsplash marble set in such a way that it looks like waves. The counter has interest with a small lamp and succulents, as well as cooking and bar supplies.

ABOVE: Sleek and modern is the order of the day here, and this is reflected in this wooden bar tabletop that cleverly overlaps the marble worktop, while lush floor-length draperies soften the overall look.

RIGHT: I adore this modern, light-filled townhouse that sits over three floors. This is the main level and although modern, it has plenty of interest everywhere you look and that is key for me when decorating any space. The generous, full drapes soften the room, along with the herringbone rug in a muted color palette of soft grays, browns, and creams. Small tables display thoughtfully edited collections of treasures old and new, while the striking ceiling light is a take on the classic Anglepoise lamp.

ABOVE: The dining area is also on the main floor and sited near the kitchen for easy serving. There is wonderful light flowing through the beautiful floor-to-ceiling windows, supplemented by the modern clear glass light fixture suspended over the table. A fully stocked chrome and brass bar cart sits nearby, allowing guests to enjoy an apéritif before dinner. The same luscious and plentiful draperies are used throughout the spaces on this floor, tying them together in a beautiful way, and picking up on the color of the upholstered dining chairs.

ABOVE RIGHT: What can I say? I am a lover of schnauzers and was giving these dogs kisses as soon as we walked in the door. They are gorgeous and look magnificent seated in this ghost chair. The perfect salt-and-pepper combination, they know the way to everyone's heart.

ABOVE: An exterior patio complete with spiral staircase looks like a wonderful place to linger on warm evenings. The party can flow outside from the living area and kitchen, with plenty of seating providing a comfortable place for guests to sit and chat. A textured rug softens the hard concrete floor and interesting wooden artwork adorns the bare brick walls, turning this space into an outdoor room.

RIGHT: The perfect eclectic mix in this pretty and comfortable bedroom. Of course the bed is the most important part of any bedroom and I always preach to layer, layer, layer—and this bed is the perfect example of that philosophy. A good reading lamp is available on both sides of the bed and I love the three panels of Asian artwork on the wall. The same muted tones that are used elsewhere in the house make for a dreamy place to fall asleep.

When it comes to choosing bedding, I always preach "layer, layer, layer."
This bed is the perfect example of that philosophy.

CHAPTER 3
CHÂTEAU

THE DICTIONARY DEFINITION
OF CHÂTEAU IS A LARGE FRENCH
COUNTRY HOUSE, WHICH FITS MY
HOME PERFECTLY. I AM KNOWN
FOR MY ECLECTIC MIX, WHICH
ALWAYS INCORPORATES FRENCH
AND VINTAGE PIECES.

The entry hall is where the massive French doors are thrown open to welcome our friends and family inside. Faded vintage rugs in muted colors layer the floor and form a welcoming mat. A mid-century chrome and glass table brings a touch of modernity into the mix and is topped with an old metal farm bucket from Budapest, filled with a plethora of blooming white orchids. French candlesticks are staggered atop vintage white books, and my prized white tufted French chairs are always center stage. Welcome to my country house.

RIGHT: I grew up with much chrome and glass, and these benches and table seem the perfect way to lighten up the hallway and add a modern touch to a house built in 1850.

LEFT: A beautiful French desk sits to one side of the hall, along with this ornate French mirror decorated with beautiful swags of molded flowers and ribbons. Modern lamps fit well here and a gorgeous silver tray is topped with many of my favorite miniature vintage finds, including a small bouquet of flowers. All my rooms have rugs with just the right timeworn qualities, never new, as well as furniture and walls in muted colors for a comforting feeling when one walks in the door.

OPPOSITE: My collection of vintage herberies (pressed herbs under glass) came from a trip to a brocante in Paris, and they add a touch of beauty to this side view of the hallway. A small Florentine table is just the right height for this urn full of white hydrangeas— my favorite flower. I have had this French sofa for many years and while you can see the patina that has come from age, I adore the shape and femininity of this piece and cannot bear to part with it.

My collection of vintage pressed herbs under glass
was a treasured find in a brocante in Paris.

LEFT: For those who have read my other books, you may remember this as the red room, as the walls were painted red for many years. I was scouring our massive attic one day and came across this abstract painting that my mother painted decades before. I thought what a shame to have it hidden away in the attic, and it sparked a total makeover for the red room, which then became peacock. I am always amazed at what a can of paint can do for a room. I love the mix of modern with vintage and the painting gave this room a whole new look, along with the deep, dramatic wall color. The gorgeous cream tufted sofa balances the large painting perfectly and the one small pillow made from a vintage floral fabric reflects the colors in the painting perfectly. Of course, everyone knows my love of trays and decanters along with vintage oil paintings, urns, and leatherbound books—all can be found here, and I think the makeover was a success.

The red room was not the only part of the house to be given a makeover. This room is the library, known as the green room as it originally had green walls and carpet, but I felt it was time for a change. The carpet was removed and the gorgeous wood floors underneath were re-polished to perfection, making the room feel much lighter, brighter, and more inviting. A white slipcovered sofa was moved down from the upstairs hall and the walls were painted a soft gray. White linen curtains are my favorite and they feature throughout most of the house. Of course I had to keep my French leather club chair, which has so much patina and also offers a comfortable seat when people visit. Once again, altering the color of the walls makes for a stunning change and is an inexpensive way to re-do any room. You will be surprised at what you can accomplish just by swapping out the paint and accessories. So often one becomes complacent when looking at the same old thing, and hopefully seeing the new version of this room will be the inspiration you need for your home makeover.

RIGHT: I adore this old cow print on canvas which we mounted to old barn wood from the property to make it even more special. The lamps in front of it light the image to perfection and the old metal dairy box that sits below it was a lucky find. A leather ottoman serves as the coffee table and a display area for my favorite glass decanters. The library is a great place to curl up on the couch for a quiet read.

RIGHT: This is the upstairs hall, which also had a makeover. I am constantly changing and refreshing rooms so that I continue to enjoy my home —it is important not to let your surroundings go stale. I have a passion for blue, and this look started with the indigo throw from Africa. I began thinking how incredible it would look as a table cover with my blue-and-white pottery. An Art Deco chest was brought in from a bedroom to serve as a display area for all sorts of blue pottery collected over the years, with a favored lamp for a dramatic statement. The oatmeal linen tufted chairs seemed to fit perfectly here, especially with the addition of the batik blue pillows that echoed the indigo throw. As always my favorite flower, the hydrangea boasting huge, beautiful blue blooms, adds to the beauty of blue that can be found here.

My lovely daughter Alexandria finished college and was moving back home for a while. Great news for me, as I was happy to have her and I wanted to make hers a room that felt pretty and sophisticated and not "little-girl pink." She has always loved France and has visited Paris with me, so it was all about French style and, of course, the comforts a bedroom should offer. The French chest has a tremendous amount of storage and I adore the curved front. It received a makeover with a muted silver coat of paint for a more modern look. We reused the fabulous French mirror and she had bought this tufted bed frame in an oatmeal linen. When your mother has a bedding line, anything is possible and Alex wanted the gray velvet. We mixed it with our oatmeal and a soft cream linen, and the finished room reflects Alexandria's style.

ABOVE: I do love putting together bouquets from our garden and sprinkling them about the house. I plucked a vintage blue Mason jar from the shelf and filled it with all shades of pink zinnias that were blooming in the garden.

RIGHT: A featherbed is plumped and fluffed on this decadent bed dressed in linen and velvet. Layers are the essence of making a bed comfy and inviting, and this bed does not disappoint.

When your mother has a bedding line, anything is possible!
Here my gray velvet is mixed with oatmeal and cream.

Our porches and outdoor areas change with the seasons. Friends and family enter through the back door, so the seating on our back porch is always decorated with pillows that go from the orange plaids of fall to reds for the holidays, and rotate with other fabrics during spring and summer. I find black-and-white tickings and checks are good any time of year. The back porch overlooks our beautiful flower and vegetable gardens, giving an idyllic outlook. The vegetable garden is brimming with rows of squash, okra, kale, cabbage, and juicy sun-ripened tomatoes. There is nothing better than farm-to-table living, and I love to cook with freshly picked produce grown in our own garden.

ABOVE: A view of our garden with vegetables, herbs, and our huge patch of zinnias that we use in bouquets all summer long.

OPPOSITE: A back porch is an ideal place to show off your decorating skills and create a relaxed space to sit and look out on the gardens. Birdcages, statuary, and vintage watering cans and buckets all become part of the mix. I hang paintings and old signs from the porch walls, and the pillows and cushions change with the season. Don't forget to add flowers and greenery, too.

IN TRUE CHÂTEAU STYLE, THIS HOME HAS ALL THE ELEMENTS OF A LARGE COUNTRY HOUSE. ONE CAN TELL THAT THE OWNERS HAVE LIVED A FULL LIFE, INCLUDING WORLD TRAVELS AND TIME SPENT LIVING IN OTHER COUNTRIES.

The owners have a passion for vintage and aged items and an appreciation of aged carved wooden pieces. The house has been brought up to date, retaining its original charm and managing to look as though it has remained untouched—an end result that we all strive for when renovating a vintage home. The use of old doors, vintage hardware, stone, wood, and backsplash options that are classic choices rather than on trend have kept the bones of the house intact.

This reception room is warm and inviting, with enormous old wooden French doors that can be thrown open to extend the party to the patio just outside. An all-neutral palette is the order of the day, and the light fixture that shines on the table is a one-of-a-kind find. These homeowners have traveled the world and have spent time living abroad so their eclectic, worldly mix comes naturally. The leather chairs have just the right patina and pair well with the beautiful antique wooden table. The whole home reflects a boho, gypsy vibe where treasured finds are mixed together in the most unique way, and we are all the better for being granted a glimpse inside.

OPPOSITE: The massive French doors make this home feel as though it is in sun-drenched Provence, perhaps surrounded by lavender fields and with sheep grazing outside. The honey-colored floors have the perfect timeworn finish that we all crave and the room comes together as a place of beauty.

RIGHT: Here we see a European-inspired kitchen with a warm farmhouse-style wood floor and simple but gorgeous two-tone cabinetry, with the green tone on the lower cabinetry setting the mood for the room. Old wooden doors with antique translucent glass and vintage handles keep the pantry items out of view in a practical yet attractive way. The stove is one designed for serious cooking since this is a family home where many meals are prepared and shared. The faucet is a work of art in itself and is obviously of restaurant quality. This is a kitchen worthy of a skilled cook.

ABOVE: A closer look at a small wooden island that is just the spot for the produce purchased in the local farmers' market. A separate tiny colander holds fresh blackberries for tonight's dessert.

ABOVE: The well-traveled homeowners have a love for
the heavily carved antique pieces that are hard to find here
in the USA. Artwork, pottery, and books complete the
dramatic look of this buffet.

ABOVE: Two young sons are lucky enough to call this their room. Soft, colorful rugs overlay hardwood floors, making them warm and kid-friendly. A grass cloth adorns the walls and gives the room a wonderfully subtle texture, enhanced by the window shades and the soft gray paint. Dark wood furniture, with a pair of matching poster beds and a rich wooden chest separating the two, set this room off to perfection. The boys' travel books are stacked on the chest, as they are always the first choice for a goodnight story around here and are dearly loved.

LEFT: Two dramatic and well-thought-out bathrooms can be seen on this page. Here a massive stone-clad shower is a fine place for a hot shower. Both rooms have natural wood cabinetry. Vintage-looking faucets and lighting make these rooms special, while a white orchid in a silver urn softens the hard surfaces.

ABOVE: Here vintage-style white subway tiles continue from walls to ceiling, while the antique light fixtures are unusual and add a masculine touch to the boys' bathroom.

CHAPTER 4 FARMHOUSE

FARMHOUSE STYLE IS ONE OF MY ALL-TIME FAVORITE LOOKS.
IT IS ALL ABOUT UTILITARIAN AND COMFORTABLE LIVING.

It is about porches for gathering family and friends to watch the fireflies at night, or for a morning cup of coffee looking over the pastureland with the rooster crowing in the background. It is a kitchen made for cooking, canning, and baking once the fruit trees start producing and the garden can be harvested, and about collecting eggs from the chicken house. Whitewashed shiplap and floors honed from footsteps that have walked across them over generations are prevalent here. Of course, every home needs a little glisten and shine, so French chandeliers provide that sparkle in many of the rooms. A picket fence surrounds and defines the yard here, and gardens burst with blooms. As the rooster crows in the evening and the sun sets in the distance, this is a place where you can take a deep breath and be thankful for farmhouse living.

ABOVE: A pristine white farmhouse sits surrounded by a picket fence in the middle of pastureland. An American flag waves proudly in the breeze, and flowers and hanging baskets welcome guests to the country.

OPPOSITE: These old barn doors can slide shut or remain open so that you can see all the way to the front porch. Here you can still hear the sound of the slamming screen door and bare feet as family make their way ouside. Old wooden pieces like the doors, the old bench that serves as a coffee table, and a timeworn chest in the front entry add to this warm and comfortable interior. This is country living at its finest.

Planting a flower cutting garden is a wonderful idea that allows you to go out and cut fresh blooms for impromptu bouquets to be used around the house.

OPPOSITE: A soft pastel-pink kitchen chair with the perfect peeling patina makes an impromptu table for showing off a sweet posy of garden roses. This home is all about repurposing, where a vintage floral coffee cup is now upcycled to become a pretty vase for roses picked from the trellis just outside the porch door.

ABOVE: A plump slipcovered sofa in a soft, muted shade of blue and tiny blue ticking pillows beg guests to take a seat. An old farm gate has been salvaged to form an interesting architectural element for the wall, framed on each side by ironstone platters. Lamp bases made from old balusters are another great way to repurpose vintage items.

RIGHT: Here the kitchen flows right into the living area and it is a kitchen that is really used for cooking. An old workbench serves as a kitchen island and as storage for all the bowls, colanders, and kitchen tools that are needed during food preparation. An old metal chicken feeder has found a new purpose as a tabletop planter so that flowers can bloom indoors. The open shelving above the stove displays the homeowner's collection of ironstone pitchers in every size. A chaise longue sits to the side, its pillow matching the slipcovered sofa seen on the previous pages, and is the perfect place for kids to sit while waiting for freshly baked cookies to be done.

This bedroom is a pale-pink confection of femininity. Beaded board lines the room in the softest shade of pink, while a French crystal chandelier twinkles from the roof beams above. It is the ultimate girly bedroom, with pink ticking and floral pillows and extra vintage quilts stacked at the foot of the bed just in case the nights turn chilly. Adding pale greens to the various shades of pink stops the room becoming overly sweet, creating a bedroom that any girl would be proud to call her own.

An old slatted metal awning has been repurposed to overhang an interior door that leads to the bathroom just beyond, where an old claw-foot tub invites you to take a long soak. Beautifully arched windows flood the room with natural light, making this a place to linger.

ABOVE: A collection of vintage cowboy boots peeks out from beneath an old bench. They not only look good, but are still worn by the homeowner, so it makes for a great utilitarian style.

ABOVE: A dainty pink bedroom hosts an all-white bed made up with vintage linens for a fresh and pretty feel. The floral accents add to the feminine vintage charm, with the antique yard-long framed floral print that hangs over the bed echoed in the floral hook rug by the bed, softening the polished wood floor. The nightstands have been painted pink to match the walls, and the same color theme is carried through to the stack of folded quilts.

ABOVE LEFT: The homeowner has scoured many a flea market for these old hand mirrors, which form a wonderful wall collection.

ABOVE RIGHT: The corner of a room has not been forgotten, and houses a pair of old slatted shutters tucked behind a pastel-pink wicker chair. Vintage floral fabric is repurposed into a beautiful chair cushion, while a metal stand holds a vintage pastel nightgown that is a darling detail in this little nook.

OPPOSITE: Who would not want to welcome the morning and brush their teeth in this adorable sink area? An antique chest in pastel pink makes a great bathroom cabinet for the bowl-shaped sink and offers great storage. Whitewashed shiplap on the wall makes a wonderful blank canvas that hosts an amazing vintage mirror, while floral platters serve as a wall accent. Even the small, old wicker trash can is a pretty decorative detail that adds to the charm of this room.

A deep claw-foot tub makes bathtime a luxury. Sited next to a window with a view, it is perfect for this farmhouse out in the middle of nowhere.

OPPOSITE: An old bead-board cabinet shows off a pink-and-white collection of retro china, while baskets hold jewelry and t-shirts. A vintage embroidered dishcloth serves as a curtain on this fabulous old door, which still boasts its original hardware. A tiny child's chair can hold essential items while one relaxes in a bubble bath, gazing out on to the rose trellis just outside.

RIGHT: This antique claw-foot tub has the original plumbing fixtures. An old wooden pillar with just the right degree of peeling paint adds architectural interest, while a petite French chandelier glistens above.

A whimsical chicken house looks as if it has always been here, but it was actually constructed especially for this spot. A long gravel path with amazing architecture (see page 8) leads to the picket fence, where a pink bicycle sports a basket of flowers. The chicken house is constructed completely from vintage elements, including old barn wood, windows, porch posts, and a great old door. It all comes together to look as though it has been here through the ages. There is a pink surprise when the door opens to reveal a cotton-candy-pink side and you meet Gloria, the female turkey who has a bit of pink about her to match the décor.

OPPOSITE: Welcome to the henhouse. The owner's love of pink continues outside, and can be found in the chicken house as a great accent with flowers, an old milking stool, and the vintage carved wooden door that is just so unexpected in a henhouse.

ABOVE LEFT: An old metal washing bin makes the perfect planter, filled with pink blooms and vibrant foliage. Vintage concrete rooster statues are perfect here, and the cobblestones lead out and around the pen.

ABOVE: The roosters strut their stuff for the ladies on this bright sunny day. They crow much of the day, as if competing with one another for the hens' attention.

ABOVE: A serene pond just outside the farmhouse is the best spot for fishing and adds to the beautiful landscape. A metal roof overhangs the side porch, adding to the welcome shade provided by lush greenery and vines.

RIGHT: The back porch is covered and quite large. Antique wooden Adirondack chairs are scattered around, while a painted bench stacked with inviting pillows provides extra seating. Old, worn, and aged galvanized metal watering cans in varying sizes make a charming collection that neatly lines the edge of the porch.

OPPOSITE: A gravel patio sits outside the front porch, and old garden elements are brought in and filled with flowers to create a welcoming spot to sit and enjoy the evening sun.

FABULOUS FARMHOUSE STYLE ISN'T LIMITED TO COUNTRY LIVING—IT WORKS EQUALLY WELL IN TOWNS AND CITIES.

You don't have to live on a farm with acres of land to adopt this style of decorating—in fact, farmhouse style can be appreciated in an apartment or townhouse with nothing more than a balcony serving as outside space. It's all about picking out the details that you can transfer to your own interior. For example, whitewashed shiplap boards can look just as good when used inside as when seen on a clapboard exterior. A porch can be appreciated anywhere, and usefully extends your living area to include your outside space, no matter the size. Decorating porches and exterior spaces is just as important as dressing your interiors, so don't overlook them—they are the first chance to make an impression.

ABOVE LEFT: A sign made from chalkboard has been set off with an antique frame. This is a delightful southern home, with the definition of a southerner appearing on the board for all to read. Vintage metalware adds to the charm.

ABOVE: Lush landscaping surrounds this small-town farmhouse, where one can hear the calming sound of running water as it streams from the fountains outside. This is a charming entry to farmhouse style and the exterior is decorated as if it were an interior, with an old window frame used as wall art. There are comfy benches, chairs, plants, urns, and everything one needs to serve a glass of sweet tea to friends who call by.

LEFT: The four antique columns in various sizes are amazing, especially the two topped with molded plinths, but the fact that they are found with all the same colors and peeling patina is striking. They look perfect tucked away in this nook and add a fabulous architectural element to the room.

OPPOSITE: A vintage iron door gets a mirrored backing to create a beautiful way to reflect the room. An old wooden desk with multiple layers of peeling paint in just the right shades of blue makes a great entry table and is filled with interesting elements displayed atop an old silver tray. Fresh flowers are grouped in an aqua-blue vase echoing the vibrant shade of blue that continues throughout the room, while the pink blooms tone beautifully with the glass baubles displayed beneath.

Silver serving pieces are stored and displayed in wonderful style with a grand French buffet that is the focal point of the room. Trays in various sizes make great display pieces in themselves when stacked together. Although hard to find, silver serving domes are something that I always hope to come across when rummaging through a flea-market table. Once used in grand homes and in the restaurant trade, they are treasured pieces in this stunning display. That is the best part of collecting—when you find yourself digging through a pile of what seems like discarded pieces in the middle of a flea-market field, and you happen to pull out a dusty, tarnished silver piece that is exactly what you are looking for, at a steal of a deal.

OPPOSITE: All sorts of silver in a myriad of styles and shapes are layered together for a beautiful visual display. An ornately carved French buffet matches their sense of grandeur, with the glass doors offering a glimpse inside of the large collection of serving pieces that have been acquired over the years.

ABOVE: Vintage shutters that have been bleached by the sun add texture and style to the bright aqua wall, hanging as a backdrop over the storage cabinet. Urns and architectural fragments make for an interesting display, complementing the weathered tones of the shutters, with the bright pink flowers adding a vibrant pop of color.

OPPOSITE: An old iron-and-wood door that was shipped over from Europe makes this corner nook something special. The tremendous amount of detail on this door makes it an amazing backdrop to the French armchair. Along with the sconce that hangs above, all elements are muted and capture the essence of French style.

ABOVE: An antique map of Paris and its monuments, picked up in a Parisian flea market, is mounted in a chic black frame and makes fabulous wall art. I love to display old maps, and I am always on the hunt for any kind of vintage advertising that is written in French—it makes for great wall art collections.

Don't be afraid to use large pieces and dramatic wall colors in
a small space, along with the eye-catching glamour of a French
chandelier dripping with sparkling beads and prisms.

Here is a wonderful example of turning a small bathroom into something dramatic. Many times in older homes—in fact, most of the time—the bathrooms are small, so they need to make a statement. Making the most of the space is key to creating a room one will remember. These elements were all collected specifically for this space and put together to create a beautiful place. The framed mirror, antique door, and stone sink all complement one another perfectly. The chandelier adds its own statement, with the amber-colored crystals picking up the tones of the wood, and just inside the closet door a peek into the collection of a favored designer's suitcases, briefcases, and satchels, stacked on a shelf for easy access and appreciation.

OPPOSITE: An elegant and sophisticated bath area is made more dramatic by vintage European elements, all linked by a color palette of ocher, tan, and cream.

ABOVE: This is probably one of the most amazing feats that I have ever heard of—the homeowner dug this basement out himself, bucket by bucket, over the years until it was complete. Now it is transformed into an amazing bar lounge and an unbelievable wine cellar, with custom-made wooden floor-to-ceiling wine racks housing an enviable collection of wines and Champagnes.

ABOVE: The bread is broken and sits on this old dough board, awaiting a generous slather of butter.

RIGHT: The kitchen has a fabulously long, antique pine table that serves as the counter, offering plenty of practical space for rolling out pie dough as well as room for the owner's collection of ironstone. A collection of ironstone platters of all shapes and sizes covers the back wall, while a wonderful wooden carved piece hanging on the wall above the table adds a warm beauty to the kitchen.

I have always loved the simplicity that ironstone dishes have to offer—there is nothing showy or glitzy about them, just an honest, hard-working beauty that pretty much sums up the essence of farmhouse style. This collection is amazing and offers all kinds of different pieces, from pitchers to platters to bowls. No cook will have to look very far in this kitchen for a mixing bowl or a serving piece of just the right size. The walls are painted a soft, muted tone to serve as the perfect backdrop for this impressive collection.

ABOVE: I have a passion for cows. Transferware decorated with cows is almost impossible to find and it is so exciting to see two of these treasured pieces in the kitchen.

OPPOSITE: This vintage metal shelf fits neatly atop this wooden shelving unit and holds an array of platters in all sizes. Pitchers are carefully selected and placed in just the right spot to show them to their full advantage. It all comes together to display the homeowner's love of ironstone and her magnificent collection.

The kitchen is the heart of any home and this kitchen was meant for cooking and gathering. Large wooden work spaces are the perfect place for making pies, rolling dough, or chopping vegetables. The antique wooden chopping block from an old butcher store looks perfect with the wood shutters offering the same honey-colored patina. An old cowbell hangs from a sturdy leather strap on the wall—an instant reminder that this is farming country. Beaded board provides a country-style farmhouse look and the mixture of bleached and timeworn woods and ironstone reminds me of home.

OPPOSITE: There is nothing like cherry season and it's the best time to bake a cherry pie. All the ingredients are gathered and the first pie has just been taken from the oven to cool.

RIGHT: An old piece of wall-mounted iron fencing is an inspired place to hang skillets. Vintage metal wall pockets that may have once had an agricultural purpose are a great upcycling idea, and the vegetables on display are both convenient to grab and pretty to look at. The old French poster of the butcher at work fits perfectly here. Old French advertising pieces are scarce, so when you find a gem, it's worth snapping up.

OPPOSITE: Shutters are necessary for protecting windows during a storm, and these old, peeling ones also add a wonderful patina to any house. The metal chairs mimic the same peeling façade, but have been carefully updated with linen cushions. The iron gate welcomes neighbors to come visit in grand style.

ABOVE: My eye gravitated toward this fountain the moment I walked through the door. as I adore vintage, peeling, crusty statuary. The moss that grows wildly about this timeworn statue and fountain is the best part of this scene, adding beautiful color as the water streams over the base and down onto the pebbles below.

CHAPTER 5 EQUESTRIAN

WELCOME TO THE HORSE FARM. THIS IS A PLACE STEEPED
IN THE OWNER'S PASSION FOR HORSES, AS SHOWN BY THE
PRIZES THAT HAVE BEEN GATHERED DURING WORLD TRAVELS.

La Pearla is an amazing horse farm. The property is surrounded by a magnificent stone fence and filled with lush woods, green pastures, ponds, and an amazing home that stretches up three stories. This is home to one of the most talented individuals I have met—he is a master at creating stunning displays, which can be found in the interiors here. An avid collector and a famed jewelry designer, the homeowner's passions also extend to interior design.

ABOVE: An enormous French mirror fills the wall that rises up three stories. Masculine leather chairs flank either side of the mirror along with some fine examples of taxidermy. An antique trunk with stickers reflecting a lifetime of travel and memories is a prized possession here.

OPPOSITE: The love of riding is apparent as one comes through the door, with saddles draped across the rail outside and also displayed inside. The new curtains are in the family tartan and look marvelous on this log wall alongside the polished leather saddles and the table made from a valet.

RIGHT: Wooden beams line the ceiling, giving way to an open atrium that allows you to appreciate the full height of this amazing house. Open landings lined with railings allow light to flood through. A grand piano on the next floor looks over this open-plan living area and when played, the music carries throughout the house. Here comfy worn leather sofas and inviting buttonback leather club chairs are dressed with the touches of plaid that reflect the homeowner's roots. Faded vintage rugs layer the floors, while a wooden cart is upcycled as an interesting coffee table. Here, as in all the other homes I visited for this book, the appreciation and passion for vintage items are immediately apparent.

ABOVE LEFT: A vintage salesman's trunk that once held shoes is repurposed as a table for the hallway. The rich blues in the pottery lamp base sit well with the vase of lilies and an ornate antique French clock. Behind these, wall art comes in the form of a transport destination sign.

ABOVE RIGHT: A large wicker trunk serves as both a table and as storage for throws and blankets during the winter months. A hat rack holds hats of both the homeowner and guests as they enter the door, and there is a collection of walking sticks to one side—part decorative and part practical. The darling dog finds a favorite resting spot.

OPPOSITE: A French leather club chair makes this entry hall a place to remember, the worn and cracked leather simply adding to its considerable charm. Wooden elements such as the mirror and the antique marble-topped table bring a contrasting warmth to the cool gray walls and tiled floor.

RIGHT: A dining area of grand size comes into its own when parties are thrown or family dinners take place here. Tall windows and doors flood the room with natural light, and allow you to appreciate views of the surrounding gardens. Beautiful silver serving pieces, sparkling glassware, crisp white linen, fine china, candlelight, and wine join forces to make for a lovely evening for all to enjoy.

This home boasts two large dining tables and this one is in the room that leads off the kitchen. After an energetic morning of horse riding, guests are invited back here for restorative mimosas and a tempting selection of fruits, cheeses, and crackers. The scene is set with the glorious bouquet that the homeowner has put together himself, placing it on a low pedestal to be sure that it draws the eye. Above the polished wood table is an unusual light fitting made from metal that replicates tree branches. To the side, a run of French doors look out on to the weathered stone walls, which give way to breathtaking views of the surrounding property.

LEFT: Oversized hydrangea blooms are plucked from the garden and gathered together in a wide silver bowl with added ferns and fruit to make a glorious display.

OPPOSITE: An antique pine hutch is filled with an impressive collection of silver serving pieces that act as decoration when not being pressed into service.

ABOVE: An artist's palette awaits the next round of painting in this inspiring studio. All the tools and equipment are at hand—palette knives and brushes of all sizes, inks for fine calligraphy, sharpened pencils for sketching.

ABOVE: The back of an antique leather club chair shows off a fine trio of beautifully crafted silver and turquoise concho belts in a unique way. The surrounding pots of plants are wrapped in humble burlap and displayed on pedestals.

Natural daylight streams into this studio from overhead and from all sides.
This room is an artist's dream, and the works created here range from
detailed paintings to exquisite pieces of jewelry.

ABOVE: The heavy beams overhead add to the interest of this
eclectic studio. Paper parasols hang from the corners, while a
round table has an unusual carved wooden base. Old and new
oil paintings intermingle, and to the side an old worktable
holds an artist's paint supplies. Here there is space to relax
and be inspired, and then to create.

The covered back porch area is also home to the wine barrels that have been brought up from the property's wine cellar and a place where wood is neatly stacked for the upcoming winter months. The cellar is a wine enthusiast's dream and this is the perfect spot to enjoy a glass before dinner. One can sit here and listen to the crickets in the nearby pond or relax to the sound of trickling water that flows in the brook just outside the door. Folding leather campaign chairs provide comfy seating, while a slatted wooden bench is piled with the plumpest of pillows.

OPPOSITE: An eclectic vignette of a delicate French chest mixed with the masculinity of snowshoes and a vintage deer head sits just inside this door. Somehow all the items work together— the sign of a confident decorator.

ABOVE: Once the horses have been stabled for the night, it is time for the finest wine to be served here. An oversized wine bottle set on a section of tree trunk acts as a conversation piece.

OPPOSITE: Stone walls surround this equestrian property in grand style, and the horses here are truly magnificent. On a fine evening, an upholstered French sofa is carried from the house to create a romantic setting for sharing a bottle of wine. Stacked vintage cases serve as an impromptu table, while an old silver tray with the perfect patina hosts a pretty bouquet of flowers. The horse grazes peacefully in the background, and a stone nymph looks on wistfully.

ABOVE: An elegant campsite is prepared as the trio of horses take a break and wait patiently by the log hitching post. A campfire set within a circle of stones burns down and waits for guests to make their way over for a feast of fine wine, soft cheeses, and the grilled fish that was freshly caught in the brook just beyond the gate here. Split logs serve as seats, with the dappled light adding to the peaceful, rustic atmosphere.

PART TWO

DETAILS &
VIGNETTES

It is my hope that this section will serve as an inspiration to all who love to design and decorate. The first part focuses on decorating with trays—I use trays throughout my home as they offer stunning and original ways to host the trinkets and trappings that you hold dear, telling a story of your life so that your home speaks of you. The final chapter is dedicated to all my friends who are living their dream and building masterpieces of art for retail consumption. Here it is all about thinking outside of the box, and these creative artists display vintage pieces in incredible ways—a must-see even if you are not in the design business, as many of these could be created in your own home.

CHAPTER 6 TRAYS & TABLETOPS 132

CHAPTER 7 MASTERS OF ART 140

CHAPTER 6
TRAYS & TABLETOPS

Trays can play a useful yet meaningful role in decorating your home. The tray instantly makes objects seem more special by giving them a platform and a defined space, and the tray options are practically endless. I have called this "tray art" as it does create such an artful vignette. I use trays of every kind, including mirrored, ornate vintage silver, wooden, shiny, matte, patterned or plain surfaces, and then top them with serving pieces, pitchers of iced tea, bouquets of flowers, or special objects that deserve to be displayed.

The trays will also give you the option of displaying items at a different height, which is always useful when creating a vignette. I constantly use trays as a way to show off objects that I collect, placing them on a coffee table or a console table to be admired by all.

ABOVE: Silver trays make the perfect platform for tabletops, ottomans, or just about anywhere. Here a pair of vintage bookends featuring a handsome pair of lions takes center stage, enclosing two leatherbound books. The wicker echoes the color of the books' bindings, while a beautiful miniature bouquet of ferns, white roses, and hydrangeas completes this vignette.

OPPOSITE: A stunning collection of Florentine trays in an array of shapes, sizes, and jewel-like colors makes a dazzling display.

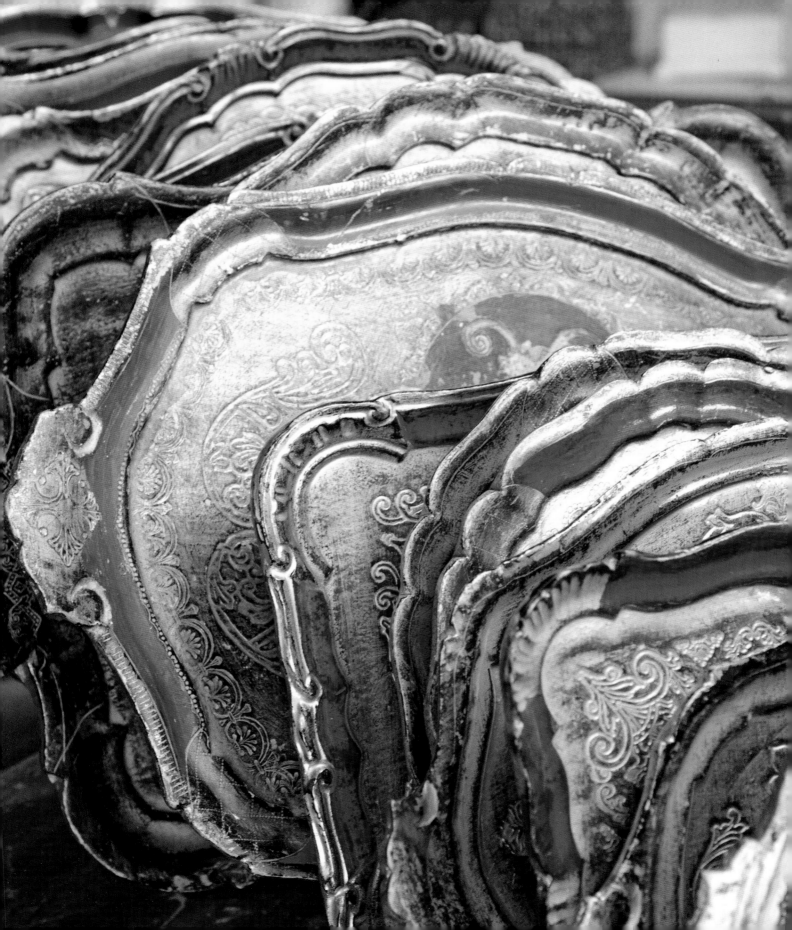

ABOVE: I adore this vintage pink pedestal tray that I picked up on a visit to Paris. The Staffordshire poodle goes perfectly with the tray and the pink is echoed in the beautiful pink peony bouquet.

ABOVE RIGHT: This tray sits atop a beautiful vintage tufted leather bench. The tray is topped with an amazing array of Vincent Peach Jewelry that is displayed in an interesting way alongside antique leatherbound books and an old candlestick. Thinking outside of the box and repurposing vintage items are key to outstanding display.

RIGHT: A vintage galvanized pedestal tray becomes a decorative stage for this collection of wicker bottles and an old, tiny lunch basket that now contains a small fern. A found bird's nest adds a bit of natural interest, while an old flower frog holds a vintage reading card printed with the word "nest."

ABOVE LEFT: I love a bar cart, and this sleek and glamorous mid-century cart is filled with fabulous liquor bottles, decanters, and all manner of bar accoutrements.

ABOVE: This mirrored bar tray sits atop a bar in a sleek Mid-Mod home. It has everything one needs for mixing the perfect cocktail, including jiggers and strainers, plus glassware and liquor bottles.

LEFT: This glass and metal two-tiered tray adds a touch of beauty to the dining area with hydrangea blossoms in the palest pink, limes, breadsticks, and vintage silver.

In this chapter I have taken great care to put together
a wide range of inspirational tray ideas that you could
easily incorporate into your own home.

I have a passion for interesting vintage leatherbound books, and by interesting I don't mean just the contents of these volumes, but the amazing bindings that can be found on these old treasures. Books are a great means of creating varied display heights within a collection simply by stacking and then topping them with interesting pieces, or even just letting the books stand alone. They can be beautiful works of art without even cracking the cover. A small vase filled with beautiful flowers adds an instant beauty to any room and always looks wonderful on a tray.

Tray art can also include a culinary twist, for example with a cheese tray that is as delicious to look at as it is to eat. Something as simple as a cutting board can become a stunning visual when layered with herbs, meats, soft cheeses, olives, and a wonderful array of fruits. Herbs of all kinds are essential for the keen cook and also smell divine as their aromas drift about the kitchen—try gathering together pots or pitchers of herbs and placing them near the stove. Fig leaves make for a beautiful backdrop for cold meats or pâté, and a trip to the garden for a ripe pear or some summer blooms can add that special something to any food tray, elevating the visual to another level.

I adore a bar cart or a bar tray, especially one stacked with antique glass decanters. You don't need to limit their use to the dining room—rather than using them only to serve a fine French brandy, try siting them in the bathroom and fill the decanter with anything from liquid soap to mouthwash. The decanters can bring a touch of elegance and class to mundane, everyday products—I have a transferware pedestal tray placed next to my kitchen sink and fill it with a small vase of fresh herbs, a beautiful decanter of dishwashing soap, and the sponge for cleaning. Not only does it look charming, it is also totally functional for keeping cleaning supplies handy.

I hope the photographs in this chapter will inspire you to use trays in a whole new way for entertaining and for decorating your home. A tray of any shape or size is so useful in elevating the look of any object it is topped with, no matter if it is a small statue that was discovered tucked away in a Parisian brocante or a generous wheel of Brie cheese, warmed in the oven and ready to be spread across a crusty loaf of bread and served with fig jam. The choices and uses are unlimited, so go ahead, experiment, and create your very own tray art.

ABOVE LEFT: This party tray has a bright orange accent with brilliant tigerlily blossoms and an old French glass jar filled with clementine oranges that spill out on to a small plate, with the label on the wine bottle also picking up on the orange theme.

ABOVE: Wooden trays are the platform for an amazing cheese board that deserves to be the delicious centerpiece at a dinner party. Freshly picked herbs are gathered into bouquets, while dried fruits, nuts, and mouthwatering cheeses and pâtés wait to be spread on a crisp cracker.

LEFT: This pretty cook's tray sits next to the stove. It is a great example of utilitarian style as well as a necessity for the cook, keeping seasonings, vinegars, and olive oil close to hand.

ABOVE LEFT: A decorative tray can be filled with all sorts of trinkets and treasures that need to be shown off. This one holds a vintage rosary, old mannequin hands, and a fossil.

ABOVE: Finding these delicate, creamy containers is a challenge and as a collector, it is like winning the lottery when you come across one at a tag sale or flea market. The small vase holds white rosebuds and an ironstone creamer is the vessel for a miniature and lacy fern.

LEFT: A butler's pantry is styled in a way that not only allows easy access, but also draws attention to the varied sizes of silver trays that are visually so pleasing.

OPPOSITE ABOVE: My favorite French perfume in bottles of all sizes and shapes creates a beautiful tray display.

OPPOSITE BELOW: In this powder room you can see a hint of the Venetian mirror, a collection of vintage Barbola mirrors in pastel colors, a candy box topped with a darling white terrier, and a rose bouquet that echoes the floral wallpaper.

CHAPTER 7
MASTERS OF ART

"Vignette" is French for a small decorative picture or display, and this is a term I have always used in my own work. After all, creating a small setting in your store is like creating a picture, an artist's personal masterpiece created with the products and pieces.

During my childhood I was surrounded by inspiration and design, with a mother who was a designer and artist. I have grown up creating, so it was no surprise that I have followed a similar path. As a child I loved treasure hunts, and as an adult I use those same skills to indulge my passion and love for vintage finds as I work my way through many a flea-market field to seek out that buried treasure. The excitement of finding something with great beauty, perhaps hidden in a cardboard box of old newspaper, something that can be brought back to life and appreciated once again, that is the ultimate recycling.

LEFT: A stunning display at the fabulous Warrenton/Round Top Antiques Week. After a buying trip to France, all kinds of French treasures were unloaded from the container and worked into a marvelous and inspiring visual display that will delight clients and passersby.

OPPOSITE: Grand horse heads look over the fabulousness of this showroom, where antiques of all kinds are celebrated. Plants, herbs, and flowers are brought in to add to the buyers' delight.

My creative side is also balanced by my entrepreneurial spirit and my business brain. I wanted to create beauty, and found that by transforming a room or creating retail or wholesale space with amazing displays was what I was born for. When I began my business, one of the things that set me apart from others was the fact that I always created elaborate room displays featuring vintage pieces mixed with our own brand of products. Other retailers did not do that. I remember being at the different wholesale marts where products were piled on tables, or even stacked on the floor. People would walk by my showroom wondering why I was going to all this trouble for display. I explained that if you wanted to sell more, you need to show retailers what to do with the products and how they can display them in their own stores for maximum sales.

OPPOSITE LEFT: A mirror is surrounded by trailing greenery and old statuary, creating a divine display.

OPPOSITE RIGHT: A vintage red iron French urn is filled with white roses that spill forth and echo the roses in the antique painting that hangs above.

ABOVE LEFT: All my favorite things can be found here— old cow paintings with the perfect patina, antique trophy cups, and an old silver punch bowl, which becomes a vessel for topiary.

ABOVE: A large antique angel statue is framed beautifully by a stack of ornately carved vintage frames, with architectural elements added in to form a breathtaking display.

ABOVE: Twice a year we can be found at the Warrenton/Round Top Antiques Week in Texas, where we pay homage to our love for antiques. Antiques are mixed together beautifully with a staggered display of pedestals, vintage spooners, silver plate, a bird's nest, aged trophy cups, and decanters. All are put together in a masterful mix.

ABOVE RIGHT: An old cow print peeks from the background and an aged silver tray is a platform for books, old wine bottles, and a pair of antlers mounted on a plinth.

RIGHT: An unusual and interesting conglomeration of an old bucket, a vintage tool belt, and hooks, along with the vintage packaging that I adore.

I take pleasure in the great detail that existed many years ago. With many of these vintage items, this kind of detail cannot be replicated in new reproductions and it makes me happy just to cherish these items once again.

In fact, just a couple of years ago, I was licensed by a huge New York showroom for big-box retailers. I was shocked that the showrooms were not decorated, so I made a list of all the things we would need to make my space look like me, which included shipping boxes of vintage props to the big city. The next season, the entire showroom was looking more like my space, so I guess they learned from my example. It seems so basic and intuitive to me, and now it appears that many others are catching on and I am always seeking out wonderful displays.

This chapter is full of those whom I consider the Masters of Art. It is for all of us who wish to take a different road, one that does not lead to an 9–5 job, but a 24/7 passion. We live for coming up with creations that consumers can appreciate. This chapter was very important to me because it is hard to find inspiring tips and ideas for creating store, booth, or tradeshow displays. Even if you don't aspire to have your own business and just appreciate beautiful things, I think this will still appeal to you as it also offers ideas you can use in your own home.

OPPOSITE: The love of pink is always a retail attraction, especially when it comes in the faded and muted tones that only vintage can provide. You can see how this display is expertly done, with a pink-and-white awning overhanging an amazing mirror, a pale-pink chest and a pale-pink satin vintage prom dress that would make anyone the belle of the ball.

ABOVE LEFT: These stacked crates make a great display box for the graceful beauty of these old concrete swan planters.

ABOVE: Another pale-pink chest is surrounded with a shell mirror, architectural elements, and flowing floral vines that contribute to an amazing retail environment.

ABOVE: A fabulous white chinoiserie chest with wonderful brass hardware serves as the perfect base for this spectacular display of blue.

ABOVE: A closer look at the framed shell art in cobalt blue and an amazing collection of blue-and-white pottery that is always eye-catching and dramatic.

ABOVE: A huge wall art design consists of framed French herberies anchored by a wonderful muted French chest and a beautiful pair of classic lamps.

ABOVE: Another French chest in a similar shade of soft gray is topped off with an ornate gold mirror and an Italian lamp, while a Florentine table supports a shell display.

ABOVE: This is an interesting tabletop retail display of an array of antiques, with a marvelous vintage steamship print, antique binoculars, leather books, and a few pieces of tarnished silver creatively grouped together.

ABOVE: A dining-room setting with a wall of antique shutters, a charming antique floral painting, and a large dining-room table and chairs, which look marvelous and are done on a grand scale.

ABOVE: A faded and distressed shade of green makes this antique armoire extremely desirable. The store display continues with polished vintage silver, stacks of old books, woven baskets, and slipcovered chairs.

ABOVE: An antique chest with a muted cream paint finish is host to a pretty pair of antique lamps, a pitcher of colorful parrot tulips, a mirror with a gorgeous carved frame, alongside a slipcovered chair.

ABOVE: Over in this little kitchen nook, I love the disarray of these fancy pieces. The linen napkin is tossed in among this rack of beautiful blue transferware and the silver pieces, looking as though someone has just finished doing the dishes.

OPPOSITE: This stack of pale-blue transferware is shown off under a glass dome, encircled by dried hydrangeas with just a hint of blue. Cloches are a great way to make anything look more special, as they act as a small glass showcase of sorts.

When you open yourself up and let the creativity and the imagination flow, anything is possible, and who knows, it might end up a masterpiece.

OPPOSITE: There is something amazing about seeing all the colors of paint in this vintage artist's box—it reminds me of getting a new watercolor set as a child. It gives you a sense of anticipation of what can be created and an appreciation of the rainbow of hues, which are a picture in themselves.

ABOVE: Sometimes I find the best way to tackle a redesign or to create a vignette is to gather all the individual elements and many times they will all start to come together naturally. The antique aquarium pictured here is amazing, and the use of shells inspiring.

ABOVE: A small French chest is ornately carved with magnificent swans on every corner. This all-white environment is a mix of old and new with statuary, stacks of candles and decanters, and a wonderful pure-white giant hydrangea that spills forth from a vintage urn.

OPPOSITE: Our slipcovers, home accessories, signature linen pillows, and antiques are showcased in this display for Carolyn Westbrook Home. The French chandelier is reflected beautifully in the mirror, and the small ornate urn that came from France is one of my favorite pieces. A more modern twist is interwoven throughout with the faux-brick white-washed wall, the shell lamps, and a chrome and fur bench.

ACKNOWLEDGMENTS

I am fortunate to have some wonderful clients who have become friends and the same with many of my amazing colleagues, whose talent I so admire. I want to personally thank each and every one of my homeowners who are clients, friends, and/or colleagues and who took part in this new book and added to the beauty.

Courtney Barton and family Thank you so much for letting us in to shoot your wonderful and eclectic home that comes from your world travels and your lovely, wandering spirit that has led you to live in other parts of the world. I always say that travel is the best inspiration and changes your perspective and allows you to bring other cultures and interest into your home. Your home is comfortable, relaxed, and all about family, with your little boys running about and their footsteps echoing across the wood floors. We enjoyed every minute of it. Courtney also is a colleague with her own store.
Mela and Roam, 4819 Blossom St. (Upper loft), Houston, TX 77007
melaandroam.com

Karen Beach Karen was one of my good customers and is now one of my dearest friends. She has a great sense of style and has a love of French things, just as I do. She is always an amazing hostess and can cook spectacular meals that always begin with a cheese tray and magnificent cocktails. Her home reflects her style, which is warm and welcoming to all guests and friends, and there is always a good time to be had by all. Thank you so much for letting us in to shoot, and for cooking and housing us while we were there.

Leslie and Bill Cornog I featured the stunning home of Jackie, Leslie's mother, in one of my other books. When she told me that she wanted me to see Leslie's home, I knew it was going to be good. Jackie is not just an antique dealer, but a marvelous designer of both interiors and displays that are jaw-dropping. I was in awe when I arrived at Leslie's striking home and once I entered, I was thrilled to be able to share it. Thank you, Leslie and Bill, for allowing us to come and photograph your beautiful home.

Julie Ferrell Julie is a darling young woman, the daughter of one of my dearest friends and colleagues, Jennifer Nicholas (Jennifer's farmhouse is also in the book). I absolutely adore Julie and her sweet family, and she let us in right before they went out of town for their summer vacation. Her style is elegant and French in a modern and relaxed way, and I can see glimpses that came from her mother's sense of style. Her home is absolutely stunning and I am so pleased to include it in this book. Thanks Julie!

Mary Francis Mary is my kind of woman. She has a get-it-done kind of spirit that I love and that good southern vibe that comes from growing up in the south. She is an accomplished and successful businesswoman and has traveled across the globe and back—and she has an elevator in her house, so who doesn't love that? Her style is a mix of her treasures that she has picked up along the way and a sophistication that comes from good taste. Thank you Mary for inviting us into your home and feeding us delicious Tennessee barbecue that we picked up down the street and consumed within minutes as it was so good. When you come to Texas, I will return the favor, my friend.

Jennifer and Jim Nicholas Jennifer and I met at the Warrenton/Round Top Antiques Market many years ago. We both have a passion for the treasure hunt and have spent much time perusing and scouring flea-market tables. She has a love of Barbola and her darling husband, Jim, has spent much time shopping with me to grab a surprise for Jennifer. I also love Barbola and would always try and have a collection of these mirrors for him to choose from. We are delighted to have Jen and Jim's farmhouse featured in the book and it showcases Jennifer's adoration of pink, roses, cowboy boots, and chandeliers. I love you both and I am so excited to show off your lovely home.

Jennifer and Dee Pepper I also know Jennifer from Warrenton/Round Top Antiques Week. We have been doing this show for decades and customers come from all across the nation, so this is a place where we love to gather twice a year. I first knew Jen as a customer and then it turns out that my friend Donna was her sister so we all became friends, which ultimately led to me turning up at Jen's wonderful home. Jen is a traveling surgeon and works much of the time. I got a sense of her style from her fabulous taste as a customer, but I was overwhelmed when I walked through the door. It is utterly amazing and I love that she cherishes vintage as much as I do. Her husband, Dee, has put much blood, sweat, and tears into this home, where he actually hand-dug the basement bar and wine cellar, bucket by bucket. They both have a love and a passion for their home that is evident as soon as you walk through the door. Thank y'all so much for letting us in and for making my book more beautiful!

Jonathan Pierce Jonathan has had an amazing life, first as a celebrated Christian singer and then opening a successful design business in Nashville, Pierce and Company. As if that weren't enough, he starred on CMT's show America's *Ultimate Country Home*, so when we discussed the possibility of his three-story townhouse being a part of my book, I was very excited. I was met at the door with his gorgeous black and white schnauzers, and anyone who knows me knows my love of schnauzers, so I knew we were kindred spirits. I felt that we would be fast friends and we were.

Jonathan and his partner, Michael, opened up their beautiful home to us and we are all the better for it. To my talented, sweet and inspirational friend, Jonathan... thank you.

Pierce and Company, 2700 Belmont Blvd., Nashville, TN 37212
www.pierceandco.com

Vincent Peach I have known and adored Vincent and his girlfriend, Michelle, for many years. Vincent is one of the most interesting and amazing people I know. He is a world-renowned jewelry designer, and his pearl creations can be found adorning many celebrity clients. He is an avid interior designer, artist and painter, singer, can play musical instruments, can fly a plane, builder and master of construction, cook, and he is one of the best merchandiser-stylists I have ever seen. We also met at Warrenton/ Round Top antiques market, when I saw his amazing ability for display and it was then that I knew that we had to be friends. We have now been friends for many years and I was so honored to be able to share his home in the book. His love for horses and nature comes across beautifully in the Equestrian chapter. Here's to my good friends Vincent and Michelle for allowing me to share their gorgeous style with the world.

vincentpeach.com or visit the flagship store at 1310 Clinton St. #107
Nashville, TN 37203

George Brownlee and Darrel Davenport These guys are part of the reason I knew that I wanted to create the Masters of Art section of the book. They are both amazingly talented, and their love of vintage and their ability to create a work of art in their display are why they had to be photographed. This is not something that can be taught, it is a gift and having the eye to know how to put it together perfectly is rare. Thanks to both of you for letting me share your talent with my audience.

George Brownlee 254.715.5712 and DLD Imports, 1001 West 34th St., Ste. D Houston, TX 77018; Darrel Davenport 832.890.0047

Jodi and Mike Roberts A talented couple who also win the award in my opinion of Masters of Art that is portrayed through their love of French style. They put together a glorious display of the best vintage oil paintings, statuary, and Florentine that their clients cannot wait to buy. Their vintage French style is undeniably fabulous, and I love just hanging out with them and taking it all in. Thanks to both of you for allowing me to showcase your talent.

Roberts Antiques 407.342.6804

Donna Corr Donna has a very vintage and feminine look that is her signature style. Her love of roses and floral in anything from vintage fabrics to aged oil paintings, from Italian and French furniture to glistening chandeliers, will make any passerby swoon. This time there was a marvelous pale-pink satin vintage prom dress that begged to be worn to the vintage prom that takes place in Warrenton at the show. Thanks Donna for a wonderful visual display.

Corrabelle Rose 517-281-1174

Ed Fulkerson and Michael Brennan of Leftovers Antiques I met Ed many years ago at a show we did in Denver, Colorado called Old Glory. Since then, he and his partner, Michael, have opened an iconic shop for those who love antique and vintage finds, and basically all things good. There are luxury bath items for both men and women, an array of design books, food items, and everything for home. It is masterfully done in a huge warehouse-sized store that is so much more than any big box could offer. I have been fortunate to have done several book signings here and they host marvelous customer parties. Thanks guys for letting us come in and photograph your masterpieces of display. If you ever down that way in Texas or if you are up for a road trip, this place is worth the trip.

Leftovers Antiques, 3900 U.S. Hwy 290 Brenham, TX 77833
Ph. 979.830.8496

I would also like to thank Cindy, Gillian, Dawn, Sally, and Louise at Cico Books for giving me the opportunity once again to create a book that we can be proud of. I appreciate all your hard work.

To Keith Scott Morton and Eric Richards for fabulous photography, as always, and our trips afford you guys some time away from New York to enjoy barbecue, country music, and a little fun along the way. Love to you both!

Maddie Ray, who took the author shot for the book—you are a fabulous young talent that I am happy to have discovered... right in my own backyard.

maddierayphoto.com

As always, I would like to thank each and every one of you who buy a copy of the book and who have supported me through social media.

And of course, thank you to my family, as without all of you, I would not be able to do what I do. Love to my husband Joe, my daughters Victoria and Alexandria, my son Nicholas, my talented and supportive mother, Charlotte, and my father, Charles. I also would like to thank my mini-me Carrington, who is my darling niece, and my nephew, Christian. Carrington is only nine years old and has a love of vintage, crafts, fabrics, and creating beauty, just like her Aunt Carolyn.

For more information, look for me on Facebook, Instagram, and our website at www.carolynwestbrookhome.com.

xoxo Carolyn

INDEX

aquarium 155
artist's box 154

bar displays 63, 105, 135
bathroom
    château style 78–9
    farmhouse 86, 88–91, 105
    maison style 29, 32–3
    tray displays 136
bedroom
    château style 68–9, 77
    farmhouse style 86–8
    maison style 29
    mid-century modern 56–7
books
    library 64
    tray art 132, 134, 136, 144
    vignettes 150, 151
bottles
    bar displays 63, 105, 135
    tray art 132, 134–5, 138
    vignettes 144, 156

cellar 105
ceramics/pottery
    blue and white 7, 66–7, 118,
      148, 152–3
    displays 34–5, 84, 91, 106,
      109
    ironstone 84, 106–9, 138
    transferware 20, 25, 26, 108,
      152–3
    tray art 134, 136, 138
    vignettes 147, 148, 151
château style 58–79
chicken house 8, 92–3
clothing, vignettes 147
collections
    displaying 34–5, 52, 76, 86,
      101
    farmhouse kitchen 106
    magnifying glasses 12
    mirrors 88
    silverware 100, 101, 120, 122,
      138

trays/tabletops 60, 63, 98,
    100, 132–9
vignettes 140–57

dining areas
    bar displays 135, 136, 137
    château style 72–3
    equestrian style 120–3
    maison style 17, 26
    mid-century modern 46–7,
      49, 54–5
    tray displays 136, 137
    vignettes 150

equestrian style 114–29

farmhouse style 80–113
fireplace
    maison style 17, 22, 25, 26,
      29, 31
    mid-century modern 42
    outdoor spaces 37, 38, 129
flowers
    château style 58, 60, 66, 68,
      70, 79
    equestrian style 121, 122–3,
      124, 129
    farmhouse style 82, 84, 93,
      98, 101
    maison style 7, 15, 17, 18, 41
    tray displays 136, 137, 138
    vignettes 143, 147, 151, 152,
      156

gardens 70, 80, 93–4, 97, 113,
    129

hallway
    château style 58–61, 66–7
    equestrian style 118–19
    farmhouse style 80, 98
    maison style 12, 20, 34–5

jewelry, tray art 134, 138

kitchen
    château style 74–5
    farmhouse style 84–5,
      106–11
    maison style 22–3
    mid-century modern 50–1
    tray displays 136, 137
    vignettes 152–3

library, château style 64
lighting
    château style 60, 79
    equestrian style 122
    farmhouse 83, 86, 91, 105
    maison style 32
    mid-century modern 46, 49,
      51, 52, 54, 56
    vignettes 147, 149, 151, 156
living areas
    château style 62–5
    equestrian style 114–17
    farmhouse style 80–3, 105
    maison style 25, 31
    mid-century modern 42–4,
      49, 52–3

maison style 12–41
mid-century modern 42–57
mirrors
    château style 60, 68, 79
    equestrian style 114, 118
    farmhouse style 88, 98, 105
    maison style 20, 25, 31
    tabletop displays 138
    vignettes 142, 143, 147, 149,
      151, 156

office, maison style 18
outdoor areas
    château style 70–1
    equestrian style 127–9
    farmhouse style 8, 80, 92–7,
      112–13
    maison style 15, 36–41
    mid-century modern 56

shells 147, 155, 156
silverware
    farmhouse style 100, 101,
      120, 122
    trays & tabletops 132, 138
    vignettes 143, 144, 150, 151,
      152
statuary 15, 18, 42, 70, 93, 113,
    143, 156
studio, equestrian style 124–5
style, eclectic mix 12–15

trays/tabletops 60, 63, 100,
    132–9

vignettes 127, 132, 140–57
vintage
    eclectic mix 12–15, 50
    renovations 72
    upcycling 111, 116

wall art
    château style 60, 63, 64
    equestrian style 127
    farmhouse style 83, 87, 101,
      103, 111
    maison style 15, 16, 20
    mid-century modern 49, 56
    vignettes 143, 149
window treatments 32, 52, 54,
    64, 77, 114
windows 32, 42, 44